Can You See Me?

Using Understanding to Help Students of
Poverty Feel Seen, Understood & Valued
in the Classroom

Can You See Me?

Using Understanding to Help Students of
Poverty Feel Seen, Understood
& Valued in the Classroom

Belinda Adams

Certified, Childhood Trauma Professional

Anchor Book Press · Palatine

Can You See Me? Using Understanding to Help Students of Poverty Feel Seen, Understood, and Valued in the Classroom. 2nd Edition

Copyright © 2018 Belinda Adams

Published by Anchor Book Press, Ltd

440 W Colfax Road, Palatine, IL 60078

ISBN: 9781949109498

Printed in the United States

Dedication

This book is dedicated to my husband and son, who tolerated me when I went back to school to become a teacher, twice, and who stood by me as I struggled with becoming the more confident teacher I am today.
I also dedicate this book to my mother, who always said I would become a teacher, even when I wasn't sure.
Thank you for believing in me!

Acknowledgements

I'd like to acknowledge first and foremost my students,
who shaped my vision of myself and taught me more than any
books I've ever read. I'd also like to acknowledge my fellow
educators, who laughed and cried along with me at successes,
misfires and failures, and Carol Pirog, who taught me how to see
students through a different lens. Thank you, my dear friend, for
opening your own heart and sharing your experiences that helped
me grow as an educator and individual.

"Teaching and learning should bring joy. How powerful would our world be if we had kids who were not afraid to take risks, who were not afraid to think, and who had a champion? Every child deserves a champion, an adult who will never give up on them, who understands the power of connection, and insists that they become the best that they can possibly be."

Every Kid Needs a Champion
Rita Pierson

Foreword

To the reader I would like to say, *Can You See Me?* presents some radical, yet simple concepts. Ideas that if we think about it, we would say make complete sense. Ideas that you can begin to incorporate in your classroom tomorrow, but you will spend a lifetime tweaking to fit your teaching style and your students' needs. Ideas that sound much like my mother as she used to reprimand me with, 'you are the oldest, you need to set the example' and that is a key. With stories that cause us to laugh and to cry, Belinda admonishes us that the first step to success is setting the example; we must change if we ever hope for our students to change.

In *Can You See Me?* Belinda shares what works. It worked for her and it can work for you. Through the years I have analyzed the data from her classroom. Working with the most difficult students, year after year, her numbers were on top. Students that had previously shown very little growth, were making 1, 2 and even 3 years academic growth. Over the years that didn't change, even with mandates from administration to use this program or that program. Granted, some curriculum was easier to use and some curriculum got better results, but Belinda's students always showed more improvement than other students in other classes using the same curriculum. Research has shown, the teacher is the most important variable that schools can control. But, as Belinda will tell you, she didn't start out that way. She had to research, learn, and change the way she managed her classroom. Fortunately, Belinda has shared that information with anyone who will listen in *Can You See Me?*

Belinda is one of the most caring teachers I know. While all the rest of us were praying that we didn't get that difficult kid, Belinda was ok with it. Not only that, and I believe this is another key to her success, she loves those difficult kids and she loves her job. Administration would be wise to look for teachers like Belinda; teachers whose kids are making progress for the first time; teachers who love their jobs. Stop in their rooms. See what they are doing. My guess? They will all be teaching differently, but the key components will be the same; the concepts you will find in *Can You See Me?* The concepts Belinda shares are things that all teachers can put into practice. Some are skills, some are strategies, and some are just how to understand and connect with your students.

For new teachers, if this isn't your first week, you have probably realized that your degree did not prepare you for life in the classroom, especially in a low-income school. For that I can only repeat what Belinda says, "...*I realized that there is NO education that can prepare you for 'life' in the* classroom. *Sure, professors might be able to 'teach' you how to teach. But they can't teach you how to survive, or better yet, how to love your job."* The concepts in this book are essential to your success and your students; they don't cost a lot of money or a lot of time, just a willingness to do what it takes to make a difference.

~ Carol Pirog, Educator, Data Analyst, Author

Table of Contents

Introduction

So, fellow educator? That's who most likely would open these pages. I want to be honest up front as I know how valuable our time is. If you're opening these pages thinking that my experiences and advice will solve your class management horror issues ... or that my insights might change those students (adults) who challenge your sanity daily ... then close this book quickly! Because I don't want to offer any false prophecies about what's inside.

HOWEVER, if you view our profession as a journey .... A continuous evolution taking place within ourselves. A humbling experience. Exhilarating moments that quicken your heartbeat. With moments (or hours) of tears either due to frustration in dealing with administrators or the challenges of your students.

If any of these ideas strike a chord for you, then I think it's worth your while to keep reading. Because, our profession is a journey! Filled with potholes as deep as valleys and moments of gratification as high as mountains that can be described by few other professionals.

If this is you … kick off your shoes and sit back with a fresh cup of coffee and an open mind, and most importantly, an open heart!

Location, Location, Location

What happens when you take a white, middle-aged, middle-class woman and make her a teacher in a low-income, predominantly Hispanic school? Confusion? Chaos? Frustration? Ding, ding, ding! All of the above!

I took my first teaching position when I was 39 years old. I'd taken many detours before unpacking my boxes (and hopes and dreams) in that small, poorly-lit classroom in an older school in the area where I had spent my childhood, where the demographics had changed dramatically over the past 20 years.

That first year, as the only English speaking first grade teacher, I joined the ranks of one English speaking classroom and 4 bilingual classrooms for each grade level in a Kindergarten through 4th grade building. I considered myself lucky to find a job in a job market that was rich with elementary school teachers and in a climate of school district budget cuts and school downsizing in the face of a dwindling housing market.

I want you to view these stories in the proper perspective. So, you'll need to have a mental image of where I teach. My school district is one of the top 5 largest community school districts in Illinois. The Fox River separates the schools and the students in more ways that you can imagine. The East Side is an older part of town, and consequently, so are the schools with tired-looking classrooms and few technological advancements. The West Side is a newer part of town, and likewise, sparkling schools filled with the newest of everything. If you haven't guessed yet, I teach on the East Side of the river. I teach where the population demographics are 95% free or reduced lunch students, families who migrate from inner city Chicago to areas of low-income apartments and homes in the suburbs.

In short, my students are poor – many of Latino backgrounds, some of African American culture, sprinkled with a handful of white students. It may seem that their cultural heritage bears little weight; that's what I thought when I started. That's what we are told. All kids are the same. I couldn't have been more wrong.

I spent four years teaching 1st grade in that small elementary school. I began with high hopes of willing and compliant students; that soon dwindled to tiny wishes of students who would, at the very least, show up for school on a regular basis and follow my directions, sometimes. Before I "wised up" to the facts of teaching students from low-income families and a culture I didn't understand, I spent a lot of sleepless nights trying to imagine ways to engage their young minds. I spent a lot more time in my classroom asking for (and waiting for) my students to "want" to learn. Unsuccessfully, of course. No 6-year-old wants to learn anything … until they begin to have fun and value what you have to teach them!

Four years later, I took my freshly-printed master's degree in special education, packed my boxes of books, bulletin board

4

borders, and posters to make my way across the highway to the 5th-6th grade transitional school with the same cultural demographics as previously, but with more African Americans coming from a low-income housing development nearby.

I spent a few years struggling in frustration in my special education classroom, those same few years trying to change the students and mold them into the "lifelong learners" every educator dreams of. Through tears of frustration, I had a revelation! Rather than wait to for the students to change (in particular, to break free of decades of poverty and years of academic failure), I realized that I needed to change. I needed to transform myself into the kind of teacher they wanted to listen to, learn from, emulate, and with the best of luck, respect!

Where to begin? I asked around. I discovered that a fellow teacher I greatly respected was a child of poverty. I picked her mind and tried to learn from her experiences. That got me started. I read a few books on how poverty impacts the lives of my students, and I realized that therein lies the answer for MY transformation. After reading Eric Jensen's candid look into poverty and children in "Teaching with Poverty in Mind" and "Engaging Children of Poverty", I started to envision just how I could begin to be the teacher these kids deserved. Eric Jensen wrote, "The reason things stay the same is because we've (educators) been the same. For things to change, we must change" (2009, p. 46).

Eric Jensen, in *Teaching with Poverty in Mind* (2009) defines poverty as "a chronic and debilitating condition that results from multiple risk factors and affects the mind, body and soul." When I look at my students, I see their individual tragedies, their struggles, their yearning for more, and most poignantly, their resilience. Many of my 10-12-year olds have seen more of life's

5

adversities in their short span of life than many, middle class adults can attest to their entire lives. They're scarred, rough around the edges, and yet, still children … yearning for acceptance and hoping beyond hope that school might bring more than additional hurt and disappointment this year.

My journey of understanding and subsequent transformation began with a candid discussion with a teacher friend, deepened while reading the words of Eric Jensen, and continued to develop as I digested more and more information about how poverty impacts children and learning. Over 15 years later, I am still learning and gaining additional knowledge and attempting new strategies with my students.

This is the point of my book, to share what I've learned along the way, what's worked in my classroom, what hasn't worked, the frustrations and the successes! I'm hoping you, the reader, will find a nugget of useful information from what I share and combine it with your own experiences to create more classrooms that are havens for all students; a place they can feel seen, understood, and valued; a place where they can come to love the journey of learning.

Chapter 1
Order from Chaos

Defining Chaos in the Homes of Students of Poverty

When students of poverty come to school, they are bringing different personal experiences that are unique to all other students. When studied by the National Center for Biotechnology Information, experts looked at the following characteristics of a typical home: 1) total number of times a child has moved physically to a new home; 2) total number of changes a child experienced in the primary caregiver, such as a parent; 3) total number of times a child experienced a change in the secondary caregiver, such as a grandparent; 4) total number of different people in the household, such as extended family members; and 5) total number of times household members moved in and out of the household (C. Cybele Raver, NCBI Center). In all instances above, children of poverty experienced a higher percentage of these occurrences than students not living in poverty situations.

In addition to higher percentages of the above circumstances, children of poverty are also exposed to more conflict in the home than students not living in poverty. The study reported that, "Protracted exposure to verbal conflict and violence between parents takes a substantial toll on children's emotional and behavioral adjustment, and is associated with higher levels of depression and anxiety and greater difficulties with social relationships with peers" (C. Cybele Raver, NCBI Center).

It is integral to classroom and student success that educators working with students of poverty understand these unique experiences, this trauma, that these students bring to the classroom and develop strategies that help them establish order in their minds, to get to the task of academic learning.

Establishing Order in the Chaotic Mind

All of the studies show that children of poverty lack the organization in their brain that children from middle/upper class homes seem to arrive at school hard-wired with. These are kids with no bedtimes, little structure or adult supervision, and when rules exist, they are usually inconsistent and at the whim of the adults in the home. Rules and routines aren't established in low-income homes that will help a child be successful in school. Often, their rules exist to keep them alive in their neighborhoods and out of harm's way in their own homes.

In addition, organization of physical space, which is taken for granted in middle class homes, is a luxury most students of poverty do not experience. I remember one little boy, named Elijah, who happened to tell me in an inconsequential conversation that he slept on the floor because there wasn't anywhere else for him to sleep. My partner teacher and I worked with the social worker and we were able to have a bed donated for Elijah. I'll never forget the look of pure joy on his face as he jumped up and down shouting, "I can't believe it! I've never had a bed before!"

We've got to remind ourselves, each and every day, that we don't have a window into these children's lives. Items of commonality in our lives, like a bed, a dresser, or even a closet, are not always the norm for these children. We can't pretend we know the homes they enter once they leave us each day. While some may say these statements are not politically correct, we, as educators, cannot ignore the facts or we will not find success in the classroom and neither will our students.

So how then is a teacher to establish order in her classroom? First, trash the posters with cute little children sitting straight in their chairs raising their hands, surrounded by the words "Classroom Rules". Just the word "rules" alone, sends these kids into a mode of rebellion.

Next, recognize that these kids live with the "rules" of home and the "rules" of school, usually polar opposites of one another. In "A Framework for Understanding Poverty," Ruby K. Payne (2013) describes these rules as "hidden rules"; kids from poverty struggle finding balance within the confines of these two sets of rules, "street rules" and "school rules". She suggests using a strategy for explicitly teaching these hidden rules.

This is how the conversation generally goes in my classroom the second day of school...

"Let's talk about rules, okay?" Groans. Complaints. Eye rolling. "You know, I don't know much about sports, so let me ask you a question: Are the rules for playing basketball the same for football?" Usually it takes about 30 seconds for someone to answer as they sit in stunned silence, wondering where in the world they found this idiot teacher. Finally, someone in exasperation will say, "No way. You can't use the same rules for basketball and football.

It just wouldn't work!" I ask, "What about soccer and baseball? Are those rules the same?" This time, they're louder with a resounding "NO!" "Why do you think that is?" I ask. "Because the games wouldn't work that way. The rules have to be different." "Oh", I say.

After I give those thoughts a few moments to settle in, I ask, "Do you think your family rules are the same as hers?" I say pointing from one student to another. The students look at one another and shrug. The amazing part is that I have them, their full attention, they're invested in this crazy conversation. Finally, we get down to the point of the conversation when I ask, "So, do you think it would be okay if we have a set of rules (or expectations) for our classroom that might be different than those you have at home?" "Yeah, why not?" they answer. This leads us into an open, frank conversation about what rules we can "live with" in our classroom to help it function best and give everyone the best chance of learning, while acknowledging these are not the rules needed to survive in the neighborhood.

This conversation has accomplished three things. First, it has affirmed them. The rules of their families and neighborhoods are not "wrong" or "bad". Second, they've learned a valuable lesson, that it is common to have different rules depending on the game or situation. Most importantly, I've accomplished "buy in" from the students.

Two additional concepts I needed to toss out were the words "rules" and "punishments". First in my mind, and gradually, in theirs. I needed to replace the word "rule" with "expectations" and the word "punishment" with "consequences." I had to re-construct my ideas about what were necessary classroom expectations required to complete the daily task of learning.

13

So, if you walk into my room today, you'll find the typical "classroom rules" sign up on the wall. With bold letters I printed in 120 point font, it says "expectations" and I've conspicuously taped it over the word "rules". It usually takes a couple of days for one of the students to ask, "What's with the sign?" or "Couldn't you afford to buy a new sign?" Those questions usually offer an opportunity for a conversation between the differences in "rules" and "expectations" and more often than not, the conversation ending with agreement that all of us can live with a few expectations in our classroom.

And yes, you read that right: I've got expectations, too. It doesn't just apply to the students. I tell them the expectations I promise to uphold and even let them add a few of their own.

My expectations for myself for my students:

- Expect me to be on time for class.
- Expect me to be ready to welcome you every day with a smile (regardless of what transpired the day before).
- Expect me to be ready to teach you something each and every day.
- Expect me to tell you why we are learning what we are learning and how you can use it to get a job, go to college, heck, get your driver's license.
- Expect me to try to take the feelings of each of you into consideration before I speak.
- Expect me to apologize when I do something wrong or break our classroom expectations.
- Expect me to be present for you, both physically and emotionally.

- Expect me to be the best me I can be every day!

After we go through the expectations I have for myself, the list we create for student expectations in the classroom looks pretty "do-able" to them.

Creating Structure and Routine Builds a Safe Classroom

It's safe for me to say that, by the time my students arrive in my classroom in 5th/6th grade, they've found school to be a great disappointment. They tend to view school as a place where failures are daily, rules are aplenty, punishments are quick, and learning is a task they can't seem to master.

Let me explain further. These kids, especially these low-income and special education students, have had 5 academic years to feel like failures. They've also given into what many experts call "learned helplessness". In Teaching Students with Poverty in Mind, Jensen (2009) explains, an overwhelming feeling that they can't learn and be successful and that if one sits back long enough looking helpless, a teacher will give up and either forget they asked you the question or tell you the answer. (p.16) Either way, there's not much satisfaction or feeling of accomplishment for students.

They walk into classrooms with teachers of middle-class backgrounds who have little knowledge of what it truly means to be "low-income" and who establish rules that seem arbitrary and ridiculous, especially to kids who go home with little or no rules to follow and no adults around to enforce them even if they had rules.

I participated in many parent-teacher meetings where the parent insisted that their child was not a problem at home. In the beginning, I did not believe the parents, but as my knowledge of the kids grew, I realized these kids were not a problem at home because they were following the home rules. It was only the school rules which were a problem for them. They don't buy into the rules of the classroom because they have no ownership of them and classroom rules do not help them at home.

Punishments are another element of school that these kids know very well. They experience them daily because, let's not forget, they have no ownership of the rules and, in many cases, don't even understand the rules or why they exist in the first place. Lunch detentions. After school detentions. All of these punishments which are doled out from teachers, and received by students with much resentment, have become part of their school experience. Therefore, these punishments mean little to them and do not serve as a deterrent for future misbehaviors. Even learning to avoid punishment seems to be out of their reach.

Lastly, learning … for most of them, they haven't yet learned "how" to be a student, how to be a functioning component of a successful classroom, or how to be a participant in learning. Without these skills, acquiring new knowledge always seems out of their reach. This is just another part of the learned helplessness to avoid punishment, so the students just don't try.

I've often been teased by fellow educators, and some administrators, for my strong sense of organization and my desire for structure and routine. While at the same time that they have teased me, they know that the most difficult of students often find success in this kind of classroom.

Organization, structure, routine. I thrive on it, and what I've learned over the course of my teaching career, is that students from poverty also thrive in an environment that is predictable. Not only does it take away some of the guesswork about what's expected of them (because the classroom expectations, structure and routines do it for them), they also experience a sense of "safety" because there are no surprises. Students in a safe environment relax and are more likely to engage in classroom discussions and take chances by sharing aloud answers when they might otherwise hold back. Payne (2013) writes: "When you are homeless or in a highly unstable living situation, all (of the common amenities that middle class individuals take for granted) *are disrupted. You don't know where your things are, routines aren't predictable-nor is time" (p. 96). Further, she states that "Routine often has a way of calming and orienting people" (p. 97).*

To create a climate where children of poverty can relax and learn, routine and structure is essential. Engage students as you set up the routine and structure together in your class. Then help students learn the routines; don't expect it to be something they should already know.

If It's Important to the Teacher

Too many times, I've heard teachers engaged in frustrated conversations about the fact that their students do not take ownership of their learning or do not seem to see the importance of learning the material being taught. They shake their heads in dismay and mutter to one another about "kids these days" and how it makes their jobs so difficult.

Well, if I said I've never been part of any of these conversations, I'd be lying. Early in my teacher career, I did my fair share of complaining about students. However, in the last several years, my participation in these conversations has changed. Instead, I seem to find myself playing devil's advocate or looking at the situation from the students' perspective.

Too many times we make the mistake of forgetting that we *already* know why education is important! We forget that these students often come from homes with parents and siblings that don't value education, and from what they've seen before they get to me, nothing has convinced them there's any value in education or school. Middle class families stress the value of education, a way of obtaining material items and status. Students of poverty come from families who don't value education, or the students

21

don't see college in their future; many can't even imagine a future for themselves, let alone one that's different than what they know. Even bright students think there is no need of working hard and planning to go to college. After all, they get their groceries from the food bank. If there is no money for groceries, and clothes that are not from the thrift store; how would there ever be any money for college? Sure, they have heard about scholarships, but students of poverty assume the rich kids probably get those.

It's up to the teachers to illustrate to the students the importance of learning, the significance of the material being taught. How they can use the information being taught each day is part of my lesson. I try to give everything a practical application or example. I break it down as simply as I can, especially those concepts that are more intricate in nature.

Sometimes, I think of it as what would most likely be the reaction of a toddler if I handed the child a quarter. While he might find it interesting because it's shiny and eventually put it in his mouth, he certainly wouldn't know its value or even what it can be used for. Keeping that in mind, students need to know the value of what they are learning, and even more importantly, what they can use it for today, tomorrow, and the rest of their lives.

It always seems that, sometime during the school year, one of the kids will ask me, "Mrs. Adams, do you like your job?" I'll laugh and respond, "Well, I must like school because I kept going back and now I have a job where I get to go to school every day!" They like that response, however foreign that concept may seem to them. I see them thinking, "Hmmm, maybe there's something to this school thing if she's been willing to do it for so long". One big difference for these kids is the expectation that they will go to college. In middle and upper-class homes, it is just assumed a child will go to college. For most children of poverty, this has not even been considered at home. We must plant the idea. One of my colleagues told me about the difference a teacher made in her husband's life. He is now in middle management at a large corporation, but this wasn't where he was headed. As a senior in high school, he had every intention of graduating and going to work at the factory where his father had worked many years. His teacher casually asked him one day where he was going to college. He said he wasn't going to college; he had already been promised a job at the factory when he graduated. The teacher was quick to tell him that with his aptitude for computers, he had to go to college. She helped him find a school nearby and he lived at home for the 4 years he worked on his bachelor's degree. One teacher changed his life forever.

Jensen discusses "The Rules for Engagement" in one of his books. He states, "You have the ability to engage every student, every day. But first, students need to believe you're on their side, not an adversary. When you're planning a lesson, ask yourself, 'Does this activity run the risk of making students uncomfortable? Could they be embarrassed if they fail at it?' Students must trust that you won't put them into impossible situations or make fools out of them" (2013, p. 25).

Never forget, they're watching everything you do. If you love and value what you teach, they'll eventually catch on. If you're not passionate about what you're teaching, they're not going to be engaged in learning. If you are not engaging the students in material they can see as worthwhile, they will continue to feel education holds little value. If you don't plant the seeds of going to college, no one else will.

23

Shaniqua: Turning a Tragedy into an Opportunity

One year, I had a 5th grade student named, Shaniqua. What makes her unique is that, unlike most students who show up excited (or shy) on the night to drop off supplies, she showed up crying! That's right! She was standing behind her father sobbing openly and clearly wishing she was anywhere but standing in my classroom!

I distracted her with taking her supplies and having her select a desk of her choice while I took the opportunity to speak privately with her father. He quickly explained that his wife, and Shaniqua's mother, had passed away while she was in 3rd grade, and coming to a new school for 5th grade appeared to be a change she felt she couldn't face. I thanked him for his honesty, expressed my sympathy, and promised she'd be in good hands with my colleague and me. As she left, I gave her a little side hug and assured her that we'd get through it together.

After the first week of school, she adjusted well to the routine of the classroom. And one thing became clearly apparent: This young lady did NOT belong in a special education classroom! She was bright, quick to complete her classwork, and the first to raise her hand during class discussions.

I contacted her previous teacher from elementary school to find out the story of how this young lady ended up in a special education classroom with a diagnosis of specific learning disability. Her teacher explained that, following the death of her mother in 3rd grade, Shaniqua had missed quite a bit of school. When she did come to school, she was withdrawn and participated little in classroom discussions or classwork. When her reading and math levels showed no improvement at the beginning of 4th grade, her team made a decision to place her in special education classes, so she could get more individualized attention in a smaller class environment. While this may have seemed like a good plan at the time, I thought the situation needed another approach.

My colleague and I met with her to tell her we'd noticed how smart she was. We were awarded with a smile, saying "I'm glad you noticed!" I explained that while we both understood the trauma she had experienced over the loss of her mother, we weren't going to let that effect our expectations of her work. I told her my goal was for her to be back in the general education classroom by the following year. Reluctantly, she looked at us as if to say, "Well, good luck with that!"

Throughout the year, there were tears of frustration on her part when she just didn't "feel" like working; however, my colleague and I kept our expectations high for her. I pushed her, prodded her, and, sometimes, held her in from lunch to complete the work I knew she was very capable of doing. Together, we made it through the school year and she progressed more than 2 grade levels in both reading and math. She was off to the general education classroom for 6th grade!

About the second week of school the following year, Shaniqua appeared at my door during my lunch time with a couple of her friends to tell me that she'd been accepted to be part of a fund-raising group in the 6th grade that took a leadership role in the school. I congratulated her and asked her to introduce me to her friends. She pointed to each, providing their name, and when it came time to introduce me, she said with a smile, "This is the teacher who kicked my butt every day last year!" We hugged, and I told her it was only done out of my faith in her abilities. She laughed and said, "I'll never forget it, and I know where to go if I need my butt kicked if I'm slacking off." I assured her I didn't think that was going to happen.

Both Jensen (2009 & 2013) and Payne (2013) discuss in their books how trauma is a daily part of the lives of students of poverty. They experience family deaths, family member incarceration, and abandonment on a daily basis. While saddening, teachers can't allow their feelings of sympathy to lower their expectations of students, especially those who need that extra prompting to develop skills and become successful. My feeling sorry for Shaniqua wasn't going to bring back her mother. My expression of compassion and empathy gave her the emotional support she needed to come to school. My high expectations and pushing her to excel is what gave her the momentum she needed to be successful.

Chapter 2
Mistakes & Misfirings to
Learn From

Our Jobs are Not Easy

"I have had classes that were so low, so academically deficient, that I cried. I wondered, 'How am I going to take this group, in nine months, from where they are to where they need to be?' And it was difficult, it was awfully hard. How do I raise the self-esteem of a child and his academic achievement at the same time?" *Every Kid Needs a Champion* - Rita Pierson (2013)

Educators have a difficult job, often made more impossible by a lack of understanding of the home lives and experiences of our students. As you'll discover while reading this chapter, our jobs result in a great deal of actions that too often backfire in our faces. If we're lucky, we learn from them.

Chaundrise: Attitude Makes All the Difference

When I first began teaching in a special education, 5th grade classroom of low income students, I made a great deal of mistakes, beginning day one. And generally speaking, those first few days (and weeks) determine the success of the whole school year. Either a teacher establishes herself as competent and trustworthy during that period of time, or she spends the remainder of the school year trying to "control" her class rather than instructing them.

My first and largest assumption that caused problems in the classroom was that the students would listen and respond to me, simply because I *was* the teacher and they were the students. Not! Most students, and particularly those from low-income homes, don't automatically give respect due to someone's status, such as a masters' degree in special education or being the adult in the classroom. Whether right or wrong on the part of these youngsters is irrelevant. While I can certainly say that my husband and I taught our son differently; he was taught to respect the teacher just because she was the teacher. However, expecting the same courtesy from these students was a huge assumption that cost me countless lost minutes of instruction and hours of frustration, both for myself and for the students.

For teachers to be successful (and respected) by students of this age and income status, the teacher has to "earn" the respect. How is this accomplished? Well, I can certainly attest to the fact that it doesn't occur simply by requesting or demanding or repeating it ad nauseum.

I recall one specific student who challenged my authority on a daily basis, creating disruption and an environment that was not conducive to learning. She didn't trust anyone, and certainly didn't trust me, much less respect and respond to me. On one occasion, I remember pushing the buzzer to call the office to have her removed (which was a far too common practice), and as we waited for an administrator to arrive, I said, "It's too bad that your behavior causes me to call the office so often to have you removed by the principal." To this, she responded, "I'm glad he's coming! It's about time I told him how sick I am of your attitude!"

Was that an appropriate way to talk to one's teacher? No. However, upon retrospect, there was quite a bit of truth in her statement. Without being able to establish rapport and gain respect of my students, I really had an attitude. Instead of attempting to rectify the situation, I'd retreated to more demands and consequences. When faced with disrespect, I'd gone on the defensive, allowing myself to be a victim and not a leader or role model.

In Jensen's (2013) *Engaging Students with Poverty in Mind,* he talks about how teachers bring the atmosphere with them that's reflected in the classroom, and it is too often given the descriptor of stress. He states, "Stress is not floating in the air like a dust particle. It is your mind and body's response to feeling out of control." Therefore, I can't put enough emphasis on developing a rapport with each and every one of your students and earning the respect to lead them.

My second assumption that created issues in the classroom was believing the students were there to learn. NOT! Let's not forget that they had already had 5 years of school to experience failure, and they had completely given up the prospect of learning anything in school. They were there because their parents told them to go, the bus arrived, and they got on. That's it! That's how they arrived, and without a little improvisation by the teacher, they were going to leave at the end of the day the same way.

That first year, these assumptions cost all of us dearly. The students lost the opportunity to learn and grow, academically and emotionally. In addition, without understanding and correction on my part, I'd added another year to their track record of failure and provided them with yet another reason to dislike school, teachers, and education in general.

Did all the students fail to learn that year? No, there were a few who made progress. You may wonder why. Some students just learn when presented with the information, regardless of the mistakes of the teacher or the disruption of other students. They're the lucky ones. However, as a teacher, we have to look at the class as a whole. Every year, 100% of the students should make progress! It's not acceptable to feel successful as an educator unless all of your students make progress.

According to Jensen (2013), establishing a positive classroom environment is monument to student success. He says, "One of the most important factors affecting student engagement and achievement is class climate and it's under your control. ... A positive climate is one of the greatest gifts a teacher can give his or her students, and in a way, this opportunity to change students' lives is a gift for us, too" (p. 51).

Kemal: You Got Anything Else Up Your Sleeve

A rational person would have remembered 'how' to provide choices to students that led to the right conclusion, especially after having raised a very precocious son. However, it seems that I became disillusioned with the notion that students will pick the 'right' choice when given the opportunity – you know, the choice that leads to learning and lets the teacher get back to instruction. This was not to be the case in my 5th grade classroom!

A student named Kemal was the one who took the teacher back to class, so to speak. He was a rough around the edges, 12-year-old, 5th grader, who'd been held back 2 years already. So, in addition to his added years of physical maturity, he had the street smarts of a 30-year-old man living in Chicago's old Cabrini Green.

I learned the hard way not to issue commands, such as "Turn to page 16 … or else!" Or else, what? I hadn't gotten that far, because I was still living under that false assumption that the teacher gives directions and the students follow. "Stop interrupting the lesson … or else!" Another mistake.

Without any malice, Kemal would look up from the paper he was doodling on and ask, "Well, what else?" I'd say, "What do

37

you mean, what else? I want you to turn to page 16." To which he answered, "I know, but you also said, 'Or else!' and I'm just asking what other choices I got besides turning to page 16?" Hmmm, not sure how to answer that, which soon became my mental refrain when it came to conversations with Kemal that year.

What was I going to do if he didn't turn to page 16 or stop interrupting the lesson? Delay the lesson even further with more commands and more classroom disruptions?

Studies have shown that students, especially those of poverty, don't respond well to commands. Often feeling as though they have little control in their own lives, if allowed, these students will attempt to take control in the classroom, even if that control is just to delay or disrupt learning. Students of poverty, like Kemal, have a psychological need to have some control; a need that cannot be ignored if our goal is for the students to learn.

Students need choices, especially those who feel they have little choice at home. However, I needed to be careful with choices. Again, another misconception I hadn't planned on: Don't give choices you can't live with! I might find myself saying, "If you can't stop talking so we can get to this lesson, you can leave the room." In the case of Kemal, he'd look me over critically from head to toe, trying to decide if he really was in the mood to hear what I had to teach today. Further, most of the time, the student didn't do either compliantly. And even if I did *finally* get the student to leave the room, I've now lost the opportunity to teach that child, and he's learned an easy way to get out of class and away from instruction (goal met for the student!). In a sense, I was rewarding poor behavioral choices by giving the desired option to leave the class and learning,

One mistake teachers often make is to settle for losing that one disruptive student to the hallway. That might be fine for the first day, giving the teacher (and class) a break from the disruption. However, in addition to the moral issue of failing to instruct that student, I've learned there's always another disruptive student more than willing to take the helm!

Based on *Teaching with Love and Logic* (2007) and finally remembering the lessons of my son, it's best to provide choices you can live with, whichever way the student decides to go. In addition, the choices need to encourage the student to make a decision that promotes learning. For example, "We're going to turn to page 16 and read together. If that's not an option for you right now, perhaps you'd like to read page 16 later during lunch." Or "I'm going to get started with this lesson and we can quickly get to the group work. However, if we continue to have disruptions, it's going to lessen the group time and it will have to be homework for some of you." While these may sound like punishments, psychologically there are different. You are giving the student a choice – it is probably the same choice they always had. However, when you say, if you don't do it you have to stay in for recess, it is perceived as punishment. When you say do you want to do it now or during recess, it is perceived as a choice, giving the student control.

If you notice, both choices result in the teacher achieving the same result. Sometimes, with particularly challenging students, like Kemal, I would pre-write a few of these choices onto post-its, and without interrupting directions, I'd quietly walk by his desk and drop off the post-it. He liked that! It made him feel special.

Kemal also liked that it didn't "call him out" in front of his friends, which is another pet peeve of students of poverty. They don't like to feel downgraded in front of their friends. Losing face with one's peers in the classroom can lead to larger issues of disrespect and disruption.

The authors of Teaching with Love and Logic (2007) call these positive principals 'Gold' statements. They state that, "Their power lies in putting responsibility where it belongs-on the person with the problem-while showing that you care" (Fay & Funk, p. 28).

Jaquan: What's That Lady Thinking?

When I met Jaquan, he was a scrawny Hispanic student whose attitude was much larger than his physical stature. He challenged everything! Even fun things! However, over time, I got to see the 10-year-old boy inside and found ways to make him smile and enjoy learning, despite his efforts in the opposite.

About mid-year, my math colleague and I noticed that his math skills far exceeded those of his fellow students in the 5th grade, special education classroom. We made plans to have him placed in a general education classroom with a teacher's aide for support.

To say that he was not excited about our plans would be a huge understatement. He made it very clear that he liked it where he was and didn't care if he was "too smart" to be there. Regardless, off he went because it was what was right for him academically.

In these situations, it's often difficult for special education teachers to accept the limited choices we have for outplacing a student to the general education classroom. We're limited by ratios and percentages of special education students to general education students. Plus we have to find a teacher that already has a teacher's aide present. These choices do not always provide us with the teacher or environment we feel would be the best fit for our particular student; however, we have to work with what we've got. So, as I'm sure you have ascertained, we weren't thrilled with the general education classroom Jaquan would go into. However, we liked the teacher's aide in that room and felt with a little explanation about Jaquan and his support needs, he could be successful in that classroom.

Despite his sometimes-difficult obstinacy to not measure up to his general education peers, he was successful. However, he often reported how he felt "slighted and judged" in the class, but went back each day anyway.

One particular afternoon, he returned from math class, throwing some papers across my desk and yelling, "Well, there's an F for me!" Asking him to calm down and talk with me, he explained that the homework assignment called for locating pictures on the internet that met the assignment requirements, printing them out, and pasting them onto a poster board for a presentation the next day. I patiently waited for the shoe to drop. "So, what's the problem, Jaquan?"

"Mrs. Adams, I'm embarrassed to tell you that I can't do ANY of that work!" I waited. "We don't even have electricity right now! Or a computer. Or the internet. Or a poster board!" Momentarily, I was stunned into silence. Not over his circumstance because I'd heard similar stories in the past. I was stunned by the assumption made by the math teacher that every student in her class had access to all the things they would need to complete the assignment given to them. After all, 95% of the students were receiving free and reduced lunch!

"Well, we will take care of that!" I assured him. The next morning, Jaquan didn't do any reading work in my classroom. Instead, he and I searched the internet, he selected his images, we printed them out and he successfully completed his assignment for math class that afternoon. He proudly displayed his work to the class that afternoon. Taking the time to listen to his concerns changed an "F" to an 'A", but more importantly, it changed Jaquan from feeling like a failure because of his lack of resources to knowing he was a student capable of doing well.

You might wonder if I spoke to the teacher about her assumption? Or if I told her how such assumptions alienate students, like Jaquan, not only from the class but also the teacher and curriculum? No, I didn't waste my time. I've seen it many, many times over the years in working with students of poverty. Our entire school had completed a book study and been part of a presentation about students of poverty and their unique needs. This teacher was present. She'd heard the information presented, but hadn't brought that cognizance to her classroom. Unfortunately for her, she'd lost an opportunity to connect with a student of poverty, instead demonstrating what the students already suspected, teachers have no idea about their lives!

Jensen (2009) warns of such assumptions and the debilitating effects it can have on students of poverty. He states, "The best thing you and your staff can do is include, include, include. Help students feel accepted for who they are, and give them all micro-niches for status by finding some tasks or narrow skills or knowledge sets at which they excel" (p. 90). Jensen (2009) also addresses how one successful teacher of poverty addressed the issue of homework. The teacher allowed five minutes at the end of class for doing homework. Jensen (2009) says, "This is an example of an accommodation that levels the playing field and shows an understanding of the world of poverty" (p. 150).

Rushing to Judgement Generally Works Against the Teacher

When I first began teaching, I felt that when you brought a student's rule-breaking to their attention, it was best to advise them of the consequence of such behavior at that time. I experienced a great deal of backlash with that approach. Students who would misbehave at the beginning of the school day would be advised they would miss recess or receive a phone call home. The result was students who either shut down completely without engaging in classwork or misbehaved even more, knowing that they were already going to be punished!

After reading *Teaching with Love and Logic*, I felt like a kid with a signed permission slip to the zoo. The authors (2007) detailed how it's not necessary to provide the student the details of the consequence right away. In fact, there are quite a few benefits to delaying the announcement of the consequence. For example, students are left pondering, and generally, working up a case of remorse while waiting for the consequence. Also, if a student is told to think about what he/she thinks the consequence might be, a student usually comes up with something a great deal more substantial than you had intended.

What a load this knowledge took off my mind. So often, I'd blurt out a consequence (such as lunch detention) without realizing that I had a meeting during lunch and would have to let the student serve the detention another day or without the cognition that I would have to deal with the problem student during the half-hour I had in the day to regroup. As is often the case with teachers who are multi-tasking a million tasks and juggling a hundred thoughts at once, I would frequently give out consequences that did not fit the rule that was broken.

For example, I can recall as a student in elementary school that the consequence for talking during work time was being told to hold up one dictionary on each extended hand in the corner for 15 minutes. How ridiculous that sounds now, I realize. And most likely, in today's climate, that teacher would be fired by the end of the week. However, the point I am trying to make is that the consequence had nothing to do with the transgression, talking. So, it had little impact on the student's decision to talk again in the future.

It's always best to have the consequences for not following expectations worked out with the students prior to any infractions. Yep, it better happen the first week of school!

Ask them what they think an appropriate response should be for a student who continues to disrupt the lesson or for a student who speaks to another student or adult with disrespect. You'd be surprised what they can come up with. Yes, some are totally ridiculous and, as I've explained to students on multiple occasions, any consequence involving duct tape is probably illegal. But other ideas are often accepted by the group, such as missing out on a preferred activity (like lunch recess or free time) for disrupting the lesson.

46

Furthermore, I've learned the hard way that consequences are best received in private. Often, I'll ask students to wait after class for a minute, so we can discuss it. Or I'll pass a post-it to the student as she leaves saying, "I'll see you at lunch to complete the work you didn't complete during class today."

In addition, consequences are best remembered for future plans of breaking classroom expectations when they are associated with the transgression. Failure to complete class work = complete your class work at another time, during lunch or after school. Talking to another student = an assigned seat away from the friend. Disrespect of an adult or peer = an apology, and for continued infractions, a phone call home.

I wouldn't be completely truthful if I said I always practice the approach of waiting to give consequences for classroom expectation infractions. I get stressed out, as we all do, or get pushed to the limit by the same student whose behavior day after day is monotonous in her relentless efforts to derail instruction. In general, my rush to assign consequences usually backfires. I forget the lunch detention or to move desks before school the next day, etc., etc., etc. Usually, it's the student who was to receive the consequence that brings this memory loss to my attention, making the consequence even more inconsequential!

Payne (2013) states, "Delayed consequences are usually more effective than immediate ones", and "The consequence has to be reasonable in the mind of the student; otherwise, he/she will see it as retaliation" (p. 277).

Chapter 3
Gaining Rapport without Losing Control

Visualizing Rapport with Students of Poverty

It isn't enough to have a plan to establish rapport with your students. It's more important to visualize what that rapport looks like. Is it a high five in the morning? Or a high-five after accomplishing a difficult task? Is it laughter in the classroom? Is it extra privileges?

Too often, I think, new teachers mistake the direction from veteran teachers about building rapport as attempting to become friends with your students. That's a mistake that's sure to backfire the first time the teacher makes a call that makes a student unhappy. "But I thought we were friends?" I've heard it before, and I've always answered the same way: "I'm not your friend. I'm your teacher. I'm your mentor. And I'm here to listen and help you in any way I can."

Michie (2009) in *Holler If You Hear Me* describes it as, *"A big part of teaching, was showing kids you care for them, and it's hard to care for people whom you always keep at arm's length" (p. 29).*

To me, rapport equates with "being present" for your students. No, I don't mean present as in your bodily form; it means being present in your mental state for your students. Every day. Day in and day out. Even those days when you've missed your morning coffee and you'd really just like a quiet day alone.

Rapport is sensing when a student is "off" and pulling her aside and asking if there is anything you can do. Rapport is smiling and offering a tale of misadventure of your own, or stories about your own children. Rapport is being ready to stop the lesson, when needed, and talk about feelings, empathy and the importance of treating one another with respect. Establishing rapport with your students, especially those of poverty, will buy a great deal of respect and hard work from your students.

Jensen stresses the importance of the teacher/student relationship with students of poverty due to the fact that they experience very unreliable relationships in their home lives. Carrying these expectations that their teacher is going to be unreliable as well can result in students with behavior problems and little to no motivation. He states, "Teachers are in an opportune position to provide strong relationship support" (Jensen, 2009 p. 87). "Students want the safety of a primary safe and reliable relationship. ...The relationships that teachers build with students form the single strongest access to student goals, socialization, motivation, and academic performance" (Jensen, 2009, p. 20).

Quintrell: The Raccoons Took My Homework

I had a student one year who, when he finally opened up, had a story to tell each and every day. Each story from this young African American boy was imparted with hand gestures and wide-eyed stares and a head full of short braids bobbing in all directions.

This particular day, my student, Quintrell, was on his way to lunch detention for not completing his nightly homework. Feeling frustrated by the lack of empathy on the part of the math teacher, he came to me with the "truth".

"It's like this, Mrs. Adams. The Raccoons took my homework!" Having heard many stories of life in the over-populated, low-income apartment complex, I prepared myself for an adventure. "Me and Jamar were heading back to our houses when we saw these giant raccoons on top of the garbage cans... Well, I started hollering and telling them to get out of there, aaaannnnd this is the part you won't believe, they jumped off those garbage cans and started running towards us. We started to run and those raccoons were chasing us down the sidewalk. This is when I dropped my backpack and my homework fell out. You don't think I was going back to get that, do you?" he stammered as he related the story half-winded and wide-eyed. "I got my backpack this morning from the sidewalk, but I have to tell you, those raccoons took my homework!"

Needless to say, he didn't serve lunch detention that day. Even if the story wasn't true, you had to appreciate his creativity and passion in relaying such an event in vivid detail.

What makes his story so remarkable is that this young man entered my classroom on that first day of school with a chip on his shoulder the size of an oak tree. He'd looked me up and down scornfully, wondering if this little, white teacher had somehow taken a wrong turn to end up at his school. He spent the first weeks of school thinking of ways to test my patience, wanting to assure me (and himself) that this school year was going to be like all the rest – him not doing what he was asked to do, going to detention, and spending his time getting into trouble and running the neighborhood with his friends.

What he hadn't planned on was me! I'd seen many students like him: they'd struggled through 5 years of school, learning very little, except that they were very good at failing, and feeling confident in the knowledge that teachers weren't there to teach them and it was only a matter of time before the teachers became frustrated with his lack of interest in class and sent him packing to detention. That wasn't to be the case in my small classroom. Because I DID care about where he came from and the struggles he had experienced, both in the classroom and out! I DID want to understand how I could help him be successful and I assured him day after day those first few weeks that there wasn't anything he could do to shock me. "We're in this together, my friend!" I'd say when I saw him struggling. "Let's figure it out," I'd whisper when he wanted to quit in frustration. And slowly, we became partners in his learning ... often with me learning just as much or more from him than I was teaching him.

His story is reminiscent of the exceptionalism of these children from low-come families. Often teachers who expect low-income students to be consistent in their completion of nightly homework often find themselves sadly disappointed. It isn't a priority for them; survival is!

In Eric Jensen's (2013) "Engaging Students with Poverty in Mind," he states: "Students of poverty are practical about what motivates them – they want the teaching to connect to their world. ... Teachers must make connections to their culture in ways that help the students see a reason to play the academic game."

We must show we care; we must make school relevant; and most importantly, we must convince students we are confident they can succeed.

Jake: "Mrs. Adams', You've Been Discriminated!"

It's Black History Month. Happens the same time every year, and somehow, we're supposed to make it meaningful, new, and interesting. Trying to plan ahead for the lesson, I wrote words on the board: Discrimination, Racism, Segregation.

Having looped with this group of students, I knew I couldn't open up the Black History Month folder on my laptop. I needed a new bag of tricks. I had to find a way to drive home a point that few of them recognized; how many thanks we needed to give to those timeless heroes like Ruby Bridges, Harriet Tubman, Rosa Parks, and Martin Luther King Jr.

My instruction began like the year before: "Let's talk about what we remember about these influential African Americans." Yada. Yada. Yada. I could see the looks on their faces. They weren't being disrespectful, but they certainly weren't engaged in the discussion. That is, until I told them I had been discriminated against, too! "What?!" They shouted as they sat up in their seats, indignant that someone could discriminate against their teacher of two years and astounded that something like that could happen to this blonde-haired, blue-eyed woman.

"Yep," I said, "that's right, I've been judged by others." I went on to explain how I felt those first few weeks teaching in the low-income, mostly Hispanic elementary school where I'd started teaching. I described the first morning I went out to greet my first-graders with a wide smile, only to be greeted by their parents with looks of doubt and pessimism. I told my students how I felt like I could read their minds as they looked me up from toe to head, wondering how in the world this white woman was going to teach their children anything! I continued to explain how the same experience had been repeated when I moved to another school to teach 5th grade. I described how it felt to be scrutinized by the African American parents who'd come to drop off their child's school supplies. Again, I felt their skepticism that I'd be able to do their child one bit of good.

My students just sat there, their mouths agape and I could see them playing the scene out in their head. We talked about what choices I had during those moments. I said, "Well, I could have sought revenge and made little Jose's life miserable because his mom doubted my capability." Still, no words came out of their mouths as they waited to see if indeed I had made little Jose's life miserable. I finished, "Instead, I chose to prove them wrong! I decided I'd do my best to teach their child, regardless of their disbelief in my ability. And I'd like to think that they changed how they felt about me as they watched their child learn to read."

"Way to go, Mrs. Adams," they shouted while pumping their fists up in the air. I smiled right back. I asked if they had the same options as I had when faced with situations where they felt judged? "Sure, why not?" they answered, filled with optimism that it really was as easy as I'd made it sound.

I know it's not as easy as I'd made it sound that day to enlighten students to a concept as complex as discrimination, but I'd like to think that day I may have planted a seed that caused a few of them to reconsider their notions of discrimination, and to reconstruct some options of how they respond to these situations. I wanted them to believe they are really the ones in charge of how situations like those conclude.

Marquise: When's Dinner?

Working with students from low income means that I often have to do a home visit with parents to talk about their child's behavior as many families don't have cars or functioning phones nor do they attend parent/teacher conferences. Word always seems to get around to the other students when I've "visited" a certain student's home.

One day shortly before spring break, one of my favorite, bright African American boys named Marquise asked, "When are you coming to my house for a visit?" Having explained several times to him that I had tried to call home on numerous occasions to tell his mom how well he was doing, Marquise had finally decided it was time to bring the good news to his front door. I answered, "I don't think I'm coming to your house." He asked, "Why do you only visit the kids who are bad?"

Hmmm. Good question! Without hesitation, he said, "I think that your whole family – Mr. Adams, your son, and you – need to come to my house and sit down and have dinner with my family at my table. What do you think about that?"

61

To be honest, I didn't know what to think. Or say for that matter! He had a very good point, and he knew it. He'd called this "caring teacher" out onto the court and given me the ball.

That night, I shared this story with my husband, and we marveled at the transformation that had occurred for this boy over the past 6 months. He'd come into school with his hoodie up, his eyes staring defiantly into mine, and prepared to make this school year just like the others: challenging the teacher and making little academic progress at all. And now, he stood before me, smiling, challenging, and inviting me to dinner!

I often wonder, did he tell his mother he'd invited his white teacher and her family over for dinner? And often ask myself, what did his mother say?

Eric Jensen stresses the importance of providing students of poverty with one huge cornerstone they've probably been missing: HOPE! (2009, p.113) Not a small bill to fill. Can't be done overnight, and honestly, with some students, hope may never come. What are some ways to build hope in children of poverty? Some of Jensen's strategies I've tried with success have been: 1. Telling them "my story", making me a person with struggles and hopes and dreams of my own; 2. Teaching life skills in small chunks with no lectures; 3. Reminding students daily that they can be successful, and more importantly, how; 4. Giving positive feedback that sets them up for future success; 5. Being prepared to throw out the entire day's lesson when an opportunity arises for students to build upon their social and emotional skills.

Making It Real

My students will tell you if there's one thing they can say about me it is: "She always makes it real!"

What do they mean by that? Well, everything! Education is real... Honesty is real ... Integrity is real ... Trust is real .... And Diligence is real!

All of these things they'd grown to believe didn't exist. Or at the very least, only existed in those new, beautiful, large schools across the river filled with white kids being dropped off by their parents after a delicious warm breakfast.

It's real in my classroom. When they don't know something, we figure it out ... together. When they don't have school supplies, I open my cabinet and hand it to them. When they struggle to pay attention because of the daily trauma they experience at home, I find ways to make school interesting and engaging enough to ward off the worries they have about home. When they want to give up, I tell them "I won't let you". When they need to talk, I listen. When they feel hurt, I offer encouragement and understanding. When worse comes to worse, we try to find the humor in our unified situation.

Sometimes, I shake my head in astonishment of the transformation some of my students make over the course of the school year. What began as a general feeling of mistrust of those in charge often ends in mutual respect and understanding. Students who started the year yelling, "You ain't gonna believe what happened?! That girl is gonna get herself beat up, that's for sure!" end the school year saying, "Mrs. Adams, do you think we can talk private in the hallway?" And I have to be ready to say "Sure" each and every time! I can't say "maybe later" or "in a minute" because they've heard promises that weren't delivered many times. One thing I always remind them is that I'll always hear them out, I just don't promise to agree with them. That always seems fair to them.

Jensen (2013) wrote, ""Brains were designed to reflect the environments they're in, not rise above them. If we want our students to change, we must change ourselves and the environments students spend time in every day" (p. 46). Jensen (2013) also writes about creating a "family atmosphere" in the classroom. He shares that a "classroom's social glue is not just an extra enhancement; it has real academic significance" (p. 42). He backs that up with significant data showing increasing academic performance when the students feel their classroom is like family.

Tasheka: When the Student Comforts the Teacher

I had a young, African American girl, Tasheka, who was part of the class I looped with one year from 5th grade to 6th grade. It's a huge understatement to say we'd made huge leaps in the trust category and I became a confidante she relied upon each day.

I was standing in the hallway the morning she arrived and told me her father had moved away while she was at school the previous day without telling her goodbye or even that he was leaving. I was standing in the hallway when she'd had a verbal altercation with another girl on the bus, leaving her feeling angry and certainly not ready to get to the task of learning.

One day, her friend passed me in the hallway and said, "I have to tell you something if it's okay with Tasheka." Tasheka walking several paces behind, passed me on the way to her locker saying, "She can tell you; I want her to." Sounded heavy. Tasheka's friend of 9 years told me in the hallway about a physical fight that had happened the day before after the girls got off the bus. She explained that three girls approached Tasheka saying they wanted to fight. She told me how Tasheka had repeated over and over, "I don't want to fight you guys. I just want to go home." It

65

didn't seem to matter as the first punch was thrown, knocking her to the ground. Her friend said she defended herself the best she could against three, older 7th grade girls while her friend ran to Tasheka's house to get her mother.

I asked Tasheka if I could see her in the hallway. I asked her if anything was injured? Did she need to see the nurse? She shook her head no. "Just a few scrapes, Mrs. Adams. No big deal. I'll live," she said with more conviction than I was feeling. I said quietly, "Do you want to talk to the principal and tell her what happened?" Again, she shook her head no. "What happened to you," I said, "wasn't right. There's never an excuse to treat someone the way those girls treated you." Sensing that I was on the verge of tears myself, I think, Tasheka reached around to give me a shoulder hug and whispered, "I know it's not right, Mrs. Adams. But that's how it is where I live." With that, she walked silently into the classroom, sharpened her pencil and sat down at her desk.

There's a point that I'd like to drive home about this interaction. While saddening, violence is a common visitor in the lives of students of poverty. They're not shocked by it like we might be. They've grown to expect it, and feel it's just a fact of their lives. As educators, we've got to put aside our own images of subdivisions that are safe to play in, and students who argue or tattle-tale. We've got to put aside our tendency to judge them for their participation in the violence. We've got to remind ourselves that sympathy won't help them learn new ways to handle their life situations. Jensen (2009) reiterates this by stating, "Talk to kids in unsuccessful schools, and they might tell you about school facilities falling apart, or about teachers who don't know the subjects they are teaching, or who lecture without bothering to engage their students, or who dismiss their students' life problems as trivial" (p. 80). Empathy is the key. And we've got to be a confidante, a strong mentor, and someone who never lets them down.

Demarco: Let's Get Rich Together

Jensen (2013) talks in his book, Engaging Students with Poverty in Mind, that students of lower socio-economic status don't think much about the future, especially in a positive light. He states, "Poverty is associated with lowered expectations about future outcomes" (p. 16). Quite frequently referred to as "learned helplessness" (first suggested by Hiroto & Seligman, 1975), Jensen (2013) states, "The more stress children experience, the more they perceive events as uncontrollable and unpredictable- and the less hope they feel about making changes in their lives" (p. 16).

Keeping this knowledge in mind, a few years ago I created an end of the year unit that "I'd saved especially for this class because I know you'll take it and run with it." I call it "The Entrepreneur in You". We spend about a week researching and writing and discussing 10 young entrepreneurs who have made hundreds of thousands of dollars or more, creating everything from sock puppets to greeting cards to homemade soap. The students got really excited reading about these young entrepreneurs! I think their enthusiasm has a great deal to do with first, discovering that kids can be rich, and second, showing that there may be a future for them outside of the negative one they may be facing now.

During the second week, the students decide on a business they would like to start. Students research other businesses similar to the one they want to start, name it, create a "mini business plan", and create an advertisement to tell others about their new business. You can almost feel the excitement as the students get more and more involved in their businesses, discussing it with one another and making plans for the future.

The third and last week of the unit, the students present their advertisements to the class. The class gets to provide positive feedback (and suggest improvements) to each student's business as long as the comments are of the productive nature.

I love this unit. I look forward to it each year. I'm often surprised by the creative ideas the students come up with, and the enthusiasm with which they tackle the project.

You might ask yourself that, even if this specific unit doesn't fit with your curriculum, is there another topic you can introduce that will generate this enthusiasm? Although, I have to stress: what kid doesn't dream of being rich? Whether it's as a professional athlete or rapper or actor, most dream of having lots of money someday. The idea is to teach while kids are working hard because they like what they are doing. One thing I have learned over the years, no matter how important the skill or topic I am teaching, if students do not engage in the material, any learning that takes place is minimal.

Jensen (2013) talks about developing engaging instruction and defines that as any instructional plan that gets students to participate emotionally, cognitively and behaviorally. Further, he says that engagement happens when teachers use methods for instruction that stimulate, motivate and activate their students. He states, "When the class's physical and emotional energy is high and flush with hope and optimism, students work harder and enjoy the learning more" (p. 36).

Jeffrey: "Sorry You Don't Have a Mute Button!"

One year, I had a student named Jeffrey. He was officially labeled "homeless", attending his 6th school in 4 years, diagnosed with ADHD although his medication was inconsistently administered, and he was reading at a first-grade level at the start of 5th grade when he arrived in my classroom. To say he was "a hot mess" would be an understatement.

He was a tall, skinny boy with a careful smile who, on days when he hadn't taken his medication, seemed to be controlled by outside hands, like a crazed marionette, regardless of his efforts to do otherwise. In addition to his constant motion, he couldn't stop talking either. He was ingenious in the ways he sought to entertain himself. He built many contraptions with erasers, pencils and a ruler. One time, his ruler became a flying projectile when his "helicopter" lost control. At least he had the forethought to yell, "Heads up!" as his ruler flew across the classroom, parting the hair of a couple of students before landing at my feet.

Often exasperated with his busyness and talkativeness, I'd say, "Jeffrey, I'm not exactly sure what to do with you." A favorite response was "Sorry you don't have a mute button to help shut me up because I don't mean to drive you crazy." Later as the year progressed, I'd often hold up an imaginary control, point it at him and mimic pushing a button. He'd laugh and do his best to be quiet for as long as he could, usually not more than a minute!

Let's fast forward to the end of the school year when Jeffrey found himself reading at a 6th grade level and headed to a specialized program to prepare students for college, called AVID, for the following year. You might wonder how such a transformation occurred? I'd like to say I waved the magic teaching wand we all wish we had, and Jeffrey suddenly began to learn; however, wish as we will for such an instrument, his change didn't occur that way.

It began with a serious conversation with him about how he felt when he couldn't control his actions and words. We included his mother because, as the adult responsible for obtaining his medication, she needed to hear it from her son. He described in heartbreaking detail how he wanted to do the right things; he just couldn't seem to do it without his medication.

I worked diligently with his mother to develop a trusting rapport where she understood this conversation (and the many to follow) was for the best interest of her son and certainly not a judgement about her inability to keep up with his medication. We worked together with the social worker to come up with a system for helping Jeffrey to remember to take his medication each day. When he forgot, it was agreed that Mom would be called and she would immediately bring his medication to school. Magically, 45-minutes after taking his medication, he'd be ready to learn … and learn he did! When he could focus, he became a stellar reader and interested in sharing what he learned with others.

Jeffrey is a junior in high school this year. He's no longer in the special education program, because with regular medication, he is able to learn and progress without intervention. He's still participating in the AVID program, which will provide him with a college scholarship upon graduation. When I hear from his mother, she can't thank me enough. I tell her, "The pleasure was all mine." And that's the truth! Watching the transformation of this young man, who worked just as hard as I did, to overcome his challenges, learn to be an advocate for himself, and surpass his wildest dreams of being a good student reminds me of why I do this job!

Did I still sometimes wish I'd had a mute button? Yep, can't lie about that. Some days were very trying indeed. However, in hindsight, Jeffrey's success couldn't have happened without his ability to describe his feelings and tell us how it felt to be him. With a mute button, his mother and I might never have known, or been able to help him.

Much of the material on students of poverty discusses the importance of developing that rapport with the students. They've got to feel as though you're on their side. They've got to know that you're in their corner, rooting for them. The same for the parents. While most data shows that often there is little participation from parents of students in poverty, that doesn't mean that we, as educators, stop trying to involve them. Jeffrey's situation wasn't solved with one phone call or one meeting. It was many meetings and phone calls over the course of the school year. Those actions have resulted in a relationship with his mother that's lasted for 6 years! It doesn't always turn out this way; however, we won't know if we don't try.

Ruby Payne (2013) puts it this way: "The key to achievement for students of poverty is in creating relationships with them. Because relationships are essential for survival in poverty, the most significant motivator for these students is relationships" (p. 101). She states further that, "When students who have been in poverty (and have successfully made it into middle class) are asked how they made the journey, the answer nine times out of 10 has to do with a relationship – a teacher, counselor, or coach who gave advice or took an interest in them as individuals" (p. 102).

Chapter 4

Making Myself a Real Person

Describing Teachers as Real People

I think we'd all agree that our immediate family members know us as "real people". They know what makes us happy, what makes us frustrated, and what makes us downright mad! They've seen you in these states of emotion. Often, we hide ourselves from our students, projecting professionalism and desiring to establish a role that encourages respect.

Well, I'd like to think that my immediate family members, especially my son and husband, have seen the "real person" in me and that they still respect me as an individual. I think, as teachers, we have to show our students we are "real people," often with real problems that arise in our lives that may or may not influence how our day is going to go.

It's amazing how compassionate students become when you share a personal story or setback you may have experienced. It's difficult to get this started because, in the beginning, students may smirk or snicker behind their hands. This is often because, initially, they feel uncomfortable and don't know the appropriate reaction. It's important to continue to share, and encourage them to share their stories as well. It's a process of reciprocation, and it doesn't happen overnight. However, in turn, it alters their view of their own lives, recognizing that other people (like teachers) have setbacks or bad experiences, and others are able to bounce back from them and continue with their day and their lives.

Born a Teacher?

I've wanted to be a teacher ever since I can recall. On my 8th birthday, my most revered gift was the stand-alone chalkboard I received. It was perfect! It stood about 4 feet tall and flipped over to reveal a magnetic whiteboard on the other side.

Hours upon hours were spent in cheerful teaching. When my friends grew tired of sitting quietly in their seats following my endless directions, I resorted to "instructing" my stuffed animals, who were much more agreeable and less apt to ask for their turn at being the teacher.

I carried the dream of becoming a teacher through most of my school-age years. However, once I graduated from high school, I drifted to the corporate world, where I landed a job making a very nice salary for a young woman with no college experience. A few years into the corporate world, I had maneuvered myself into the role of "corporate instructor," teaching engineers how to prepare presentations for clients.

When that role again led me again to dream about becoming a teacher, I headed off to community college and then a four-year college. And yet, even with that determination and childhood dream, it would be 10 years before I stood at the front of my own classroom, teeming with 34, squirming, giggling first grade students. A few years later, I found myself a special education teacher for a group of reluctant, 11-year-old students.

I tell this story to my students usually within the first 2-3 days of school. They hear about how I started and stopped going to college 3 times; how I graduated with a bachelor's degree only to stay home for 8 years to be a mom to my son, Austin; how I went back to school again when I was 37 and again when I was 42; and how all of these decisions led me to be right where I am today – standing in front of them as their teacher. Someone usually has the boldness to ask, "Geez Mrs. Adams, you musta' gotten bored, that's why you quit going." And I respond, "No, I missed school so much and I liked it so much, that's why I kept going back!"

Jensen (2013) states that when "...the teacher is so strongly committed to engaging students that there's a palpable 'whatever it takes' attitude in the air. Passionate, committed teachers do not accept failure as an option. They are constantly 'selling' students on themselves, the content, and the learning process" (p. 26).

Ishawna: Faith in My Schoolbag

I'd like to preface this story with the statement that there are all types of religions, and this story isn't about being religious. I included this story to illustrate a concept. If you work with children, you have to take risks, and you have to do what you believe is best for the students. Sometimes, there's an emotional price to pay for taking those risks. A parent may say hurtful things. A colleague will ridicule your efforts. A principal will call you to his office. When this happens, you have to reflect upon the situation, and if you still feel that conviction, just learn to let it go.

It wasn't as if I'd made a conscious decision NOT to bring faith to school. I mean, I said my morning prayer every morning, asking for God's blessing on my day, praying for my family's safe return that evening, and giving thanks for my many blessings.

But somehow, I discovered later, I'd been leaving faith in the car. Having had the rules about "no religion in the classroom" drilled into me since college, I'd always been very careful to avoid talks of God's existence and angels and all of that. But did faith stop there?

As with most faith epiphanies, mine came after being hurt. It hadn't been a day too much different than any others in my 5th

grade, special education classroom of mostly students from low income housing and Hispanic students. One girl, in particular, had been giving me quite a run for my money lately. Almost overnight, she'd become disrespectful, sullen and often falling asleep in class. I was worried. She had so much potential, and I hated to lose the little bit of foothold I had gained over the past four months. So, taking her aside as the others filed off to lunch, I asked quietly, "What's going on with you lately?" No answer, just eyes looking down at her scuffed-up sneakers. "Is it something at home?" Still no answer. "Why have you changed your attitude about school?" I waited. She continued to gaze at her shoes. When I was just about to give in to frustration and send her on her way to lunch, a small voice said, "I guess, I've been spending too much time with my cousin." "How so?" I asked. Another long pause. "Well, we go on Facebook and listen to music and my Auntie lets us stay up as late as we want." I wondered aloud, "You're not doing anything bad with your cousin? Like drugs?" Quietly, she answered "No" and "I'll try to do better." I thanked her and with that, sent her off to lunch, not realizing what landslide I had started.

The next morning, I was called down to the principal's office where my student sat with none other than her mother. I greeted her, as we'd had many occasions to talk about her challenging daughter and my efforts to help her be more successful at school. Mom didn't respond, and the principal went on to explain that Mom wasn't happy I'd asked her daughter what she does with her cousin, and more specifically, if drugs were involved. I did my best, relying on my most "politically correct" use of words to explain my genuine concern for her daughter and sorry if I had crossed a line. After 10 minutes of her venting, I apologized again and slunk off to my classroom.

I cried on the way home that day. Wondering why I bothered to try at all. Wondering why I didn't get a nice, quiet teaching job teaching middle-class first-graders how to sing "Jolly Phonics". I vented to my husband and cried a little bit more and spent the majority of the night tossing and turning and replaying the Mom's angry words in my head over and over.

In the morning, I stared at my tired face in the mirror and questioned my sanity for going back to school, but off I went anyway, feeling as though I was trudging off to battle.

On my way to school, I began my usual morning prayer, only I felt prodded to add a little bit more. My mom had always said that God doesn't give us more than we can bear, and that we need to turn things over to God. So, I did. As simple as that!

I told God about the previous days' events, my intentions, my hurt over the mother's reaction, and then said, "I'm laying these things at your feet, Lord. I'm letting it all go. And I'm ready to be there for my students today with your support."

But it wasn't as simple as that. I won't kid you about that. Several times throughout the day, I found my mind traveling back to the sting of the mother's words. Each time, I'd say to myself, "No, Lord I gave that to you. I'm not going to dwell on it." And I'd move on with the day. Finally, that long day was over. As I prepared my classroom for the next day, the phone in my classroom rang a call in from the outside. I answered and what transpired next changed my faith forever!

On the other end of the receiver was the student's mother. At first, I feared the worst: maybe there were a couple of choice phrases she'd forgotten to say to me the day before. Instead, I heard, "Mrs. Adams, I called to apologize for my behavior yesterday. I realized last night how awful I felt about our conversation and I wanted to say 'thank you' for caring enough about my little girl to ask those hard questions. You are a blessing! And I just wanted you to know that."

Stunned, I hung up the phone and sat down at my desk and put my head in my hands. WOW! God had *really* taken my burden and not only helped me through the day, but also opened the heart of my student's mother. I could have spent all day worrying and fretting and reliving every ugly detail. I could have been online looking for teaching jobs in white, middle-class suburbia. Instead, I'd given it to God and I'd received something so wonderful in return.

That day, and every day since, I know that I can't leave my faith in the car. I've got to pack it in my schoolbag, take it out and wear it on my sleeve, and never be afraid to let someone know I care. And when things don't work out as I planned, I know my faith will help me let it go.

Jensen (2013) writes that whether you believe in a religious God or not, it's important to question yourself and challenge yourself to be best teacher you can be. He states, "Sometimes, we're reluctant to change ourselves out of fear of risk or loss. But although taking risks may result in failure, not taking risks guarantees failure. If you refuse to try new things, you rob both your students of their possibilities and you of your own potential" (p. 174).

Jayden: Full Circle

My first year teaching I had a small classroom in a low-income school teaming with 34 wiggly, first-graders, mostly Hispanic, a handful of African Americans, including one curly-haired nymph of a little boy. To say I learned many lessons that year would be a complete underestimation of the situation.

What happens, though, when over 10 years later, I received an email from that curly-haired little nymph who had just graduated from high school? "Mrs. Adams" he wrote, "I've never forgotten you and the way you used to make us laugh and all the things you did just to get us to read a book and do our math. I'd love to see you and tell you all about the things I've done. I'm off to college in the fall. I just wanted you to know that. Do you think we could meet?"

Well, after I'd stopped crying, I quickly sent back an email with my phone number and said "Give me a call. I'd love to see you!"

My mom wanted to go. She couldn't believe I was meeting a student I hadn't seen for 10 years – a student who remembered me from 1st grade. I waited impatiently for him to arrive, searching the crowd coming towards the coffee shop. From far across the street, I caught a glimpse of bobbing, curly hair, and instantly, I knew it must be him!

Amazed, I listened to Jayden's story of all the events he'd experienced after being removed from his mother's care to live with his grandmother. He talked about his struggles to find a balance between loving a mom who hadn't been there for him and wanting to make his grandmother proud. I smiled. And he said, "What? I know you're thinking something ..." I said, "Oh, kiddo, I'm sure you make your grandma proud every day. Just look at you!" He'd smiled and said, "You always used to say things like that!" Had I? I didn't remember. What I remembered was being a frazzled first year teacher with squirrelly students who seemed to find a million ways to test my patience. So, I asked him what he remembered most about that year. Well, to hear him tell it, he remembered every day.

He remembered our daily "Hokey Pokey" before lunch, the read-alouds after lunch to a bunch of kids who had never heard a story read aloud before, and our daily afternoon release to "Who Let the Dogs Out?" He laughed and said, "I'm pretty sure we were the only class in the whole school who left every day barking!" Well, he's probably right about that.

He talked about how he'd often wondered aloud, "I wonder what Mrs. Adams' would say?" as he pondered life's questions. He said he felt I had been with him all those years.

This young man reminded me of all the reasons I'd gone into teaching! He reminded me of touching that one heart, of impacting an individual's life without even knowing you've done it. I'm so thankful for the opportunity to know that I actually accomplished that goal – for some teachers, we may touch young lives and never know it!

While we may never know, it's best to remember this young boy whose heart was changed forever. It's difficult for us, as educators, to see possibilities to include fun activities with difficult, fast-paced curriculum and administrators with unrealistic expectations. Yet, two minutes of a fun activity, like Hokey Pokey for a six-year-old made all the difference to Jayden and probably other children as well. Further, sending kids home on a positive note does a lot to improve attendance as students look forward to returning the next day.

Common sense tells us these are things that young children enjoy, and it's clearly visible on smiling, laughing faces. Research says these things also improve academics and a student's ability to learn. Jensen (2013) says that research has determined that music enhances self-discipline, brain function and increases verbal memory (p. 52). I can't be certain of all the why's and how's, but I can attest to this: the kids like it; it can change their attitude towards school; and it increases their motivation to learn. Jensen (2013) states, "Until you make your school the best part of a student's day, you will struggle with student attendance, achievement, and graduation rates" (p. 4).

Chapter 5

Stories You Wouldn't Believe But You Just Can't Make This Stuff Up!

Jessica: Is That Scratching I Hear?

There are those defining moments in life. You know, those moments that underline and add an exclamation mark to your situation. In my case, it was the definition of my job description.

The day of my defining moment began like any other. Starbucks coffee! Straggle through traffic. Make my way to my second home, the classroom, and await the arrival of the buses. It wasn't until later that I realized the enormity of the day…

It was a little past lunch and there it was again. That faint "scratch, scratch, scratch". I thought, don't panic, it's in a cage. Grade a few more papers and then the silence. A silence that was more like a freight train rushing towards me! No more scratching. What could that mean? Did it get out? I couldn't compel myself to look in the cage for fear I would be face to face with it … or worse yet, see the cage empty! Immediately, images of a small, furry creature with claws and sharp teeth scaling my leg onto my desk sprang to mind. Breathe. Wait a few more seconds. Ah, there it is, more scratching and a sigh of relief. It was only later that I asked myself, "When did scratching in a cage become the norm for me?"

Okay, before I answer that question, I'm sure you want to know what was in the covered cage in the corner by my desk?

93

Charlie, the ferret of course! Am I a teacher at a veterinary school? Good guess! Is it the day for show and tell? Another good guess. Nope, I'm just your run of the mill special education teacher in a low-income school. That event, as it turns out, was just another one of those things they don't (or won't) teach you in college.

You've probably heard the phrase that special education students often appear to be "marching to their own drummer". Well, it doesn't mean anything until you live it, every day!

As it turns out, "the day of the ferret" as it has become known, was the day of speeches in communication class. Unbeknownst to myself OR the communication teacher, one of my students had decided to give a speech about her ferret and just happened to bring it along as her "prop". No one ever figured out how she actually got the cage past the school bus driver, but when the bell rang, I was greeted with a gratified smile from my student and a cage, complete with a scratching ferret who didn't seem quite so pleased to be in the 5th grade.

Well, we all survived the "day of the ferret" including the ferret, and my student received an "A" for her efforts! That was the moment I realized that being a school teacher looks nothing like the advertisements or the depictions of bookworm teachers in horn-rim glasses instructing a class of smiling students while everyone sits in orderly rows and waits for directions. Nope, the "day of the ferret" changed my idyllic notions forever!

That day I realized that there is NO education that can prepare you for "life" in the classroom. Sure, professors might be able to "teach" you how to teach. But they can't teach you how to survive, or better yet, how to love your job and send your students home each day with a smile and an attitude that they're ready to return the next day even when they bring scurrying, furry, clawed friends to school.

Marco: "It Might Be in Something Wet"

It was early in the school year, probably the 2nd week, when my cell phone was stolen from atop my desk. I noticed it was gone immediately upon returning to my desk after dismissing my students at the door for the day. Panic swept through me! I didn't have it password protected, and the thought of my students reading my personal text messages with my husband, or making obscene phone calls to my mother or my sisters sent shivers of horror up my spine.

I quickly replayed the last few moments of class, and determined that three students had been in proximity of my desk prior to dismissal. I immediately called the parents and explained that my cell phone may have accidentally been taken by their child. Two parents agreed to speak with their child when they got off the bus and would let me know if they located the phone. However, on the third call, the student answered the phone instead of the parent. I sensed that the student seemed to have some reservation in speaking with me about the phone, insisting much too loudly that she knew nothing about it. When asked if her mother was home, she mumbled something about not knowing and hung up.

I went to the office to speak with an administrator about the problem. The principal and I drove to the student's house and were met at the door by the confused parent who had been home the whole time and didn't know I had called. We questioned the girl I spoke with on the phone, and eventually, she said, "I'm not sure if it was your phone ... yours is green, right? ... well, I'm not saying it was yours, but Marco had a green phone he was showing kids on the bus on the way home today."

The chase was on! The principal and I drove to Marco's house, and much to our dismay, he said he knew nothing about a green phone. While we waited, Mom searched his backpack and reported that there was no phone inside. There was nothing left to do; the principal and I went back to school. I spent a sleepless night, wondering and fearing which of my students might be writing down my entire contact list!

The next day, the principal took Marco to her office to talk more about the cell phone. Well, there's something to be said about trying to "interview" a special education student with lower cognitive abilities. One has to be cognizant of the fact that you cannot make the questions too complicated or ask questions that require only a "yes" or "no". As the principal later reported, she learned both the hard way as she relayed the conversation verbatim.

"Marco, have you seen Mrs. Adams' green cell phone?" "Yes." "Do you remember seeing it yesterday on her desk?" "Yes." "Did you take Mrs. Adams' cell phone off her desk?" "No." "Do you know who might have taken her cell phone?" "No." "Marco, do you think you might know where Mrs. Adams' cell phone is?" "Yes ... maybe." "Is the cell phone at your house?" "No."

Seeing this conversation was going nowhere fast, she said she changed tactics to sentence starters. "So, Marco, if Mrs. Adams' phone was somewhere, where might it be?" "Well, it might be in some...water." Knowing that this conversation could go on forever as there are endless places of water between the school and his home, she grabbed his coat, called his mother and put him in her car to take him home. As they got out of the car, she said, "Show me where Mrs. Adams' phone might be in water." With hesitation, he walked a few steps and pointed into the storm drain.

Fast forward to her knock on my classroom door. Looking elated, she held up her hand with my phone resting on her palm and said, "I've got your phone! That's the good news! There's some bad news, however ...," she trailed off. By this time, I noticed that my phone was sitting in her hand on a paper towel and that water was dripping through her fingers.

"Where did you find it?" I asked. She explained that after Marco had pointed into the storm drain, she'd looked inside and saw the shine of my bright, neon green phone resting on a ledge about 4 feet down into the storm drain. Not to be outdone by any future administrator in years to come, she'd called the public works department to retrieve my phone with a net!

While I'd like to say I was saddened by the loss of the phone, I was happier to learn it wasn't in the custody of any of my students, and my sister and aunt were safe from prank phone calls, at least for the time being.

Interestingly, when the principal phoned the parent the next day to advise her that my phone would need to be replaced and the sum I would have to pay, the parent showed up an hour later to pay me with cash for the replacement of the phone. Not wanting little Marco to get off without consequence, his mother agreed that he should clean lockers before school for the next month.

And I'd learned a valuable lesson, put a passcode on my phone so that even if it's stolen, it can't be opened and the contents remain safe. Furthermore, upon reflection, when a student strolls by your desk 3 times in one day to say, "That's sure a nice phone, Mrs. Adams'," be sure to put your phone in a safe place!

Lakesia: When Student Cell Phones Run Amok

One year, I had an African-American student named Lakesia. She had made it very clear from the first day of school that her mother was an individual to be feared should Lakesia feel slighted in any way by her teachers. She once sat through an administrative observation of my instruction sniffling and blowing into an entire box of Kleenex simply because I'd moved her seat closer to the board so she could see better since she had lost her glasses. While the observation went great, the principal who observed me couldn't resist his curiosity to ask, "What was with the girl crying in the corner?" I was a little naïve to think he wasn't going to notice, I guess.

One morning, she was assigned a lunch detention as a result of spending her class work time chatting with her neighbor rather than working. Smart students figured out quickly that they could complete their work in record time the first 10 minutes of detention and still make it out to recess. Wish I could say that all of them figured that out, but I'd be lying. Anyway, I digress from Lakesia.

Upon hearing about her lunch detention, she demanded to use the classroom phone to call her mother. When asked why she wanted to call, she wouldn't respond; however, it was pretty clear to me that she was going to report the lunch detention as a contractual infraction to her mother. After I had responded with a "no" on two occasions and she became quiet, I wrongly assumed the conversation was over and the consequence had been accepted. Not the case!

About 5 minutes before the end of the class, I noticed that Lakesia had her personal cell phone out and was dialing away. I approached her and asked her to hang up the phone. To which she responded, "I won't and you can't make me. I'm tired of you people (teachers) pushing me around." I held out my hand and again asked her to hang up the phone. Upon seeing the outstretched hand, she took the still dialing cell phone and slipped it down the front of her shirt! Yes, that's right, down the front of her shirt. With the volume fully up, we hear mom answer "Hello" and Lakesia begins to yell down into her shirt, "These people are pushing me around! They're killing me! I can't take it anymore!" Of course, mom's hysterical response was "Who's killing you? What's happening?" All the while, Lakesia just kept repeating the same incoherent statements.

The ridiculous image of this story is that, of course, no one was touching her, let alone killing her, and 4 adults (including myself, my teacher aide, and the teacher, and teacher aid from the class next door who had arrived to help upon hearing raised voices) stood helpless to either disconnect the phone or re-assure mom that everything was all right. After a couple minutes, mom disconnected the call.

Immediately after the call disconnected, I sent the class to lunch without Lakesia, left her with the other teacher and found my administrator. I quickly explained what had happened, and alerted her to the fact that the mother was most likely on her way to school to verify that her daughter was alive. This particular administrator, who was well known for her calm demeanor, shook her head with a smile and said, "You know, Mrs. Adams, I've had a lot of situations arise in classrooms with students and teachers. However, I've got to say that I've never had anything remotely like this happen before. We'll handle it together." So much for me running back to the safety of my classroom and taking refuge while the principal explained the issues which arise when students do not follow school rules about cell phone usage.

As predicted, mom arrived within 10 minutes of the phone call and we met her at the door. To ease her fears, I quickly said, "Everything is okay. Lakesia is fine. No one has harmed her. Can I explain what happened?" After this registered, Mom listened as I explained the situation, and then asked to see her daughter to confirm that she was indeed still alive, I guess.

Even though the mother understood the violation of school policy about the usage of cell phones, she felt her daughter had the right to tell her mother about her lunch detention, regardless if it was during class time. Both my administrator and I felt that the illogic in that statement couldn't be argued with and decided to leave well enough alone.

There really is no moral to this story. And I'd like to say that that was the last time Lakesia threatened to call her mom about consequences, but that wouldn't be truthful. She continued to threaten us with that one until the last week of school. I guess, it's prudent to say that not all situations can be solved with logic and clear-cut expectations. I'm sure you have noted, it's apparently impossible to hang up a cell phone (even with 4 adults present) when said cell phone is inside the student's shirt. Further, some days it's just best to go home and hope the next day will be better.

Dacquan: "Who's that Dude?"

I've discovered over the years that students in poverty rarely have a filter on their tongues. If they think it, they say it. At first, I found it a bit shocking; however, after a few years, it became pretty refreshing. Usually, there's no guessing what she's thinking because she's probably already told me that "I really should have thought twice before wearing *those* shoes with that outfit!" Being a blunt, straight-to-the-point person myself, I came to expect them to say what they thought, and encouraged them to share their feelings (in a respectful way, or at least, a way that seemed respectable to them).

Teaching in a Title 1 school equates to close scrutiny from District Administrators. It wasn't uncommon for upper level assistant superintendents to stroll into the classroom, looking for evidence of expected instructional practices. Usually, these visits were brief, and the students learned, over time, to ignore their presence.

On one particular day, my 5th graders were playing a review game on the Smart Board. After selecting the correct response, each student was allowed to call on the next student to come up to the board to answer the next question. We were not fazed by the appearance of the Superintendent of the district when he came into the room and took a seat at the back of the room, especially since they were having a great time with the activity and the chance to play "teacher" by calling on the next student.

Dacquan was a lanky, African American boy from a family of nine children. He was the oldest at 12 and the youngest was a newborn. He was often tired and difficult to engage due to the disruption of his sleep by crying babies and toddlers refusing to go to bed. However, on this particular day, he was engaged in the activity and frantically waving his hand to be called upon to go to the board. After another student was called each time, he would mutter, "That's the one I knew!" but continued to wave his hand when the next student was about to be called.

Finally, Dacquan's name was called. He swaggered his way up to the Smart Board, grinning, as he'd already located a question he knew the answer to. He quickly selected the right answer and turned around with a smirk, looking around the room to choose the next student to participate. With the Superintendent sitting behind me, it seemed like hours passed as Dacquan milked the moment of playing "teacher," watching his classmates raise their hands and plead with their eyes to be called on next.

I sighed. At last, it seemed he had made his selection as his smile grew even wider. Pointing above my head to the back row, he said, "I pick that Dude in the suit! That is, if he thinks he knows the answer ..." All heads in the class swiveled to take in the Superintendent, sitting with his mouth open, wondering if he was, indeed, the "Dude" being called upon. The students were silent as their heads swept from the back of the room to the front, taking in Dacquan's huge grin, my expression, and waiting to see what the Superintendent would do.

As I started to mumble something about choosing an appropriate student to come up next, the Superintendent couldn't resist the challenge from Dacquan. He walked up to the board and selected a question to answer. When he got it right, Dacquan held up his hand for a high-five and said, "Way to go, Dude! By the way, I sure like that suit!" All the Superintendent could think to say was, "Thank you." Soon after, he left the classroom.

Jensen (2013) relays that it is important to give students more control over what happens in the classroom. He states, "Letting students make decisions leads them to feel more engaged because they have a personal stake in the class's proceedings. When they're coming up with and acting on their own ideas, they feel empowered and excited to follow through" (p. 42).

Kemal: Is She for Real?

Earlier in this book, I wrote about Kemal, stating that it was quite a year of entertainment and challenges that year with the twice-held back from grade promotion, Kemal in the room. I could probably fill an entire book with just the antics of Kemal and the conversations that ensued before, during and after instruction, but usually right in the middle!

Part of my reading instruction included daily independent reading when students could choose their own books to read. While I had quite an extensive library in my classroom, students could also bring in books from home or one they had selected from the library. There was one requirement: the book needed to fall within the student's reading level ranges that were determined by quarterly assessments. Students were provided with reading level ranges and that assisted them in selecting appropriate materials to read. Generally speaking, this procedure went along without a hitch, that is, until Kemal made a special request.

One Monday morning, Kemal came in with a thick, black book tucked under his arm and placed it in his desk. I'd forgotten about the book until it was time for independent reading. Kemal went over to his desk and extracted the book he'd brought in earlier that morning. When asked, "Kemal, what book did you bring in to read for independent reading?" Kemal responded, "The Bible". Stunned momentarily, I finally found the words to ask, "The Holy Bible?" Kemal responded, "Well, is there any other kind?"

I started everyone else on their rotations and called Kemal over to my desk. I carefully explained that reading the Bible for independent reading was not going to be an appropriate choice for him. "Why?" he asked. I showed him his reading level ranges in his folder, and explained that the level of the Bible exceeded that range by about 500 points (or 4 grade levels!). I reiterated the reasons we read books within our leveled range is to increase reading comprehension and to avoid frustration. Afterwards, he seemed all right with my explanation, walked to his desk and put the book back inside. Wow! I smiled as I found myself thinking, that was easier than I had expected.

Later that day, the Principal stopped in the classroom to drop off some paperwork. She asked the students how their day was going and most responded with a "great" or "good" but Kemal had something on his mind. Raising his hand, he waited to be called upon and asked, "Did you know that Mrs. Adams is the anti-Christ?" My mouth fell open just about as quickly as the Principal's, who turned to me with a face that questioned the kind of instruction I'd been doing that day! I whispered, "You're going to want to hear this story." She called Kemal over and asked for an explanation. "All I wanted to do was read the Holy Bible for independent reading, and she won't let me! I'm pretty sure she worships the devil or something otherwise why would anyone say that!"

By this time, the Principal was having a very difficult time keeping a straight face and had completely forgotten why she'd come into the classroom in the first place. Smiling at Kemal, she said, "I'm sure Mrs. Adams has her reasons, Kemal, and I'm going to leave it to her to explain it again." With that, she left the room, chuckling aloud and smiling over her shoulder. Thanks for nothing, I thought.

Even though I went through the whole explanation again, and expressed that I appreciated his honest thoughts, I can't be sure if I ever convinced Kemal that I was not secretly worshipping the devil. But he took the Bible home anyway.

Jensen (2013) would describe Kemal's security in the classroom which was demonstrated by sharing his real thoughts that day. I didn't become angry at his outburst or chastise him after the Principal left. I made him feel secure in his ability to continue to share his thoughts in the classroom, both with me and others. Jensen (2013) states, "Lasting positive climates are not predicated on having 'good' students; they are thoughtfully planned and consistently orchestrated by caring, savvy professionals" (Jensen, p. 51).

Epilogue

It's a Brave New World, Mrs. Adams

To say that I spent a vast portion of my life "sheltered" would be an understatement. I'm the baby of six, protected (though tormented) by my siblings and whisked into the loving, protective home of my police officer husband when I was twenty-six. I wasn't totally oblivious. I mean, I lived with a man who fought the "bad guys" and arrested people. I vaguely remember the stories of small children, which registered but never really hit home until I became a parent myself.

These days, as my son heads off each day to his college classes, I recall his years in elementary school with fondness. There were those teachers that I loved almost as much as he did, and Mrs. Knox was one of them. She was my son's 3rd grade teacher, and probably, the first teacher in his early academic years to see him for the "gem" of tenderness and caring he really was!

She wrote something in her introductory letter home that I will never forget. As she closed her introductory letter, she penciled, "I promise to treat your child the way that I hoped each teacher treated my own children". Wow! Powerful words! A promise she lived up to that year, and a statement that planted a seed in my heart that, to this day, continues to grow.

115

Often, as I look around the classroom of my thirteen, special education, low-income students, I stop and think about the words of Mrs. Knox. Through her special "lens", no longer do I see the grungy kids with dirt under their fingernails. Instead, I see the wonder that fills their eyes when I tell a story that reveals to them I'm a person just like them. I see their wanton need to feel smart, loved, and successful. And that's my goal for each day: that each of them goes home with warmth in their heart, a funny story to tell about their teacher, and a success to share about what they learned today!

And what have I received in return? Oh, more than words can express! I've learned that the efforts I put forth today multiply tenfold over the course of the year as these students discover the power of knowledge and the strength each one possesses inside!

Good teaching requires that teachers often look critically around the classroom and ask:

- *Can students see themselves reflected on the walls? On the bookshelves? In the curriculum itself being taught?*

- *Do students feel as though their individual voices are being heard? And respected?*

- *Are the creative energies of each student being pulled to the surface?*

- *Do the students feel a connection? To their teacher? To one another?*

~Dear God~

I want to teach my students how to live this life on earth,
To face it's struggles and its strife, to improve their worth.
Not just the lesson in the book, or how the rivers flow,
But how to choose the proper path wherever they may go.
To understand eternal truth - and know right from wrong,
And gather all the beauty of a flower and a song.
For if I help the world to grow in WISDOM and in GRACE,
Then I will feel that I have won, and I have found my place.
And so, I ask your guidance, God, That I may do my part
For character and confidence, and happiness at heart.
                                        ~Amen

By Anonymous

Parting Thoughts on Poverty

It's been several years since I authored the First Edition of *Can you See Me?* I've had many more experiences since then as an educator which led me to write additional books focusing on trauma in the young child and how trauma negatively impacts students in the classroom.

Many studies have shown that poverty is traumatic. It negatively impacts the development of the brain, just as trauma has shown to do. This is significant because 21% of children in the United States live below the national poverty threshold of less than $25,500 a year for a family of four (Rocheleau, 2019).

As demonstrated by the stories of the children in this book, living in poverty often equates to an enormous amount of stress, and children of poverty exhibit different brain development than that of their peers not living in poverty or trauma. It's documented by several studies that chronic stress, such as poverty, can result in an atrophied brain, and in particular, the hippocampus part of the brain.

This lack of development in the hippocampus part of the brain is extremely important to school performance because it regulates emotional responses and plays a critical role in how the brain formulates memory and spatial awareness (Dobrin, 2012). The American Psychological Association wrote about the behavioral and emotional problems that children of poverty face. Behavioral issues often include impulsiveness, difficulty with peer relationships, physical aggression, diagnosis of poor attention and conduct disorders. Emotional issues often include anxiety, depression and low self-esteem (APA, 2019). Many of these problems are evident in the stories in this book.

One 2015 study concluded, "The poorest children showed the most delays in brain development and had the lowest academic achievement scores" (Rocheleau, 2019). While this information is helpful in understanding why some children of poverty fail to meet the academic benchmarks compared to their middle-class peers, it takes strategies like those illustrated in this book to reverse the negative effects of poverty on the brain and positively impact their future academic achievement and emotional regulation.

Article author Rocheleau states that some of the negative impact on the brain can be reversed through "education and positive interactions with parents" (2019). Teachers have little involvement in how children interact with their parents, and as I've written in this book, it's impossible to control or even know all of the interactions our students face when they leave us each day. We've got to rely on the strategies we can incorporate at school, such as building rapport, developing a school/home connection, and focus on appropriate instructional techniques that support our students in a way that encourages them to want to learn.

I'm going to be transparent. Throughout this book, I've written about fellow teachers who have not shown empathy or understanding towards students of poverty. I've included myself in several of those stories to illustrate that none of us as educators is perfect. If anything, we learn from our mistakes and misfirings, and come out on the other side as better educators and better people, too. The first time I read Eric Jensen's book on poverty, I participated fully with our school's plan for a group book study. When that book study was done, I filed his book on the shelf and went back to business as usual. Which was not always pretty. I struggled with non-compliant, disrespectful students. I struggled because my students were not progressing academically.

It wasn't until I went searching for answers to solve my classroom problems that I discovered I had the power to change my classroom. As I've told teachers who dread each school day: "It's not like the buses will be coming from another part of town today. We're going to be getting the same students we had yesterday." We cannot wait for our students to change if we want to see results and maintain our sanity, and most importantly, continue to love our jobs. Change isn't easy for any of us. However, when you start to see results in positive changes in your students, you become energized and empowered to try more and more strategies.

In conclusion, I want to remind you that poverty is very real to the children who live it every day! As educators, we have the power to negate some of its effects and help students overcome the deficits poverty may bring to their education. It is possible. The stories of my students should provide hope for future students.

Real Questions & Real Answers

Often, I've found myself in discussions with teachers, parents or administrators, and they've asked me questions that may be helpful to share here:

Q: Do you really believe that all students can (and want) to learn?

A: Yes, I do! Students are hungry for knowledge, although many of them just don't know it yet. Share a couple of interesting facts with them, such as how jelly fish reproduce or why I hate spiders but know they are necessary for our environment, and you'll have them asking for more information. Take those opportunities to open a book or look something up on the internet. You'll find you've opened a whole new world for them.

Q: What's the most important thing you've learned about difficult students?

A: The students who work the hardest to be disliked, usually through disrespectful or aggressive behavior, are the students who need to be liked the most. If we set ourselves up to be the purveyor of "like" that they've never experienced before, we usually discover an entirely different child underneath. Also, it's those same students who try my patience and cause me to grit my teeth that also bring tears to my eyes when I say "good-bye" to them at the end of the year.

Q: Do your strategies always work?

A: Generally, not the first time…lol. I usually have to tweak them and mold them to my audience. What works one year for classroom management may not work the following year. Classes each year are like snowflakes – there's no two alike. And in that vein of thought, the strategy that worked last year might not work this year without making a few modifications to allow for differences in student personalities and classroom climate. Still, even after tweaking, some strategies just are not successful with my students. That's when I've got to be willing to throw it out and start again. In general, though, most strategies will work if you're willing to devote the time and energy to fully implement them and give them time to succeed or fail.

Q: What breaks your heart the most about teaching at-risk children?

A: Children who are put against impossible odds, forced to grow up too quickly, and missing out on the pure joy of being a child. Yes, again, I may be looking at this from my own middle-class background; in this case, there's nothing wrong with that. While I cannot provide my students with the home life I had, I can build into my day opportunities for them to play, discover and enjoy just being a child without any worries.

Q: How do you feel when teachers think you're too involved with your students or think you spend way too much time working on individualized assignments or making accommodations?

A: Actually, I feel sad for those educators because they don't realize what they are missing. Without that extra effort, those educators may never experience the pure joy of watching a previously failing student find success for the first time in their school life. Those teachers will never know if they could have made a difference for a struggling student; they'll never know if they could have learned something new in the process of teaching their students something new. Teaching is reciprocal. I've found that I've learned just as much from my students as I've taught.

Q: What do you do about feeling burnt out by the extra work or never ending needs of your students?

A: Sometimes, I cry. Sometimes, I'm just so overwhelmed by the tragic home life of a student that I just can't help but cry. But crying won't help them. I often talk, and strategize with a fellow educator, or pick the brain of the social worker, counselor or psychologist. I try to leave it at school (when I can) and re-group and refresh for the next day. When I am with that child or children, I give them everything I've got, no holding back. If I've done that each and every day, I know that's all I can do.

Bibliography

American Psychological Association. Effects of Poverty, Hunger and
  Homelessness on Children and Youth. 2009.
  https://www.apa.org/pi/families/poverty

Dobrin, Arthur, D.S.W. The Effects of Poverty on the Brain: The brains of
  poor children are atrophied but can rebound. Psychology Today,
  October 12, 2012. https://www.psychologytoday.com/us/blog/am-
  i-right/201210/the-effects-poverty-the-brain

Fay, Jim & Funk, David. *Teaching with Love and Logic*. The Love and
  Logic Institute, Golden, CO, 2007.

Jensen, Eric. *Engaging Students with Poverty in Mind*. ASCD, Alexandria,
  VA, 2013.

Jensen, Eric. *Teaching with Poverty in Mind*. ASCD, Alexandria, VA, 2009.

Michie, Gregory. *Holler If You Hear Me*. Teacher's College, Columbia
  University, New York, NY, 2009.

Payne, Ruby K., Ph.D., *A Framework for Understanding Poverty: A
  Cognitive Approach*. aha! Process, Inc., Highlands, TX, 2013.

Pierson, Ruby. Every Kid Needs a Champion.
  https://www.ted.com/talks/rita_pierson_every_kid_needs_a_cham
  pion/transcript

Raver, C. Cybele, Blair, Clancy, Garrett-Peters, Patricia and Family Life
  Project Key Investigators. *Poverty, household chaos, and
  interparental aggression predict children's ability to recognize and
  modulate negative emotions. National Center for Biotechnology*

Information, U.S. National Library of Medicine, 8600 Rockville Pike, Bethesda, MD 20894 USA.
https://www.ncbi.nlm.nih.gov/pmc/articles/PMC4682352/

Rocheleau, Jackie. How Poverty Shapes a Child's Mind and Brain. BrainFacts/SfN, October 14, 2019.
https://www.brainfacts.org/neuroscience-in-society/law-economics-and-ethics/2019/how-poverty-shapes-a-childs-mind-and-brain-101419

About the Author

Belinda Adams is an elementary teacher. She has degrees in psychology and special education. She has taught students in kindergarten through eighth grade. She has taught general education students, students in special education, and students in regular education who needed remediation. With success rates that exceed expected yearly growth, Belinda is always available to discuss solutions for those dealing with difficult students because she believes every student *wants* to learn when provided the *right* motivation and support.

Belinda devotes hours each year reading new studies and books about trauma, poverty and helping children find success in the classroom. She is a certified as a Childhood Trauma Professional She's presented to her peers on the topic of accommodating special needs and at-risk students in classrooms. She continued to build her knowledge base by attending conferences and seminars, and she's always interested to learn from her peers about best practices that bring results.

Before becoming a teacher, Belinda worked in the business world and wrote a weekly editorial for a northwestern Illinois newspaper. In her spare time, oh wait, Belinda is a teacher and an author, she doesn't have spare time. She lives in the Midwest with her husband, her son, and her dogs, Murphy & Suzy Q.

Other Books by the Author

Belinda's Award Winning and Top Selling Book:

Can You See Me?
> *Using Understanding to Help Students of Poverty Feel Seen, Heard & Valued in the Classroom*

Don't Look Too Closely:
> *What Children of Trauma are Hiding and How You Can Be the Difference for Them*

If Only She Knew:
> *Engaging the Whole Student with Trauma in Mind*

Mom's Gift:
> *No Problem Is Too Big for Mom & Me*
> (Children's Picture Book)

Parents REACH for Success:
> *4 Strategies to Give Your Child the Growth Mindset for School Success*

REACH for Success:
> *4 Strategies to Positively Impact Your Classroom*

There's More to Me Than She Can See:
> *Engaging the Whole Student with Trauma in Mind*

Why Math? Mental Anguish to Humanity:
> *Engaging At-Risk Students in Math and Science When the Teacher Hates Teaching It*

Future Books by Belinda Adams

Can You See Me Yet?

This is follow-up book to Belinda's award-winning and best-selling book about children of poverty. She shares her proven classroom strategies that have helped students of poverty overcome the disparities of living in traumatic environments. Using evidence based theory from researchers of children and poverty and what she has learned after over 15 years of teaching, Belinda applies her practical strategies to help all children learn and grow, both academically and emotionally. Can You See Me Yet takes the foundation introduced in her first book and works to increase the knowledge and understanding of educators so they can fully understand the negative impact of poverty for children; in this way, attempting to bridge the gap for these students.

Throw Away Kids

When most see those three words, it is the low-income and foster care situations that probably come to mind first. That is NOT what this book is about. Special education colleagues and diligent advocates for students with special needs, Carol Pirog and Belinda Adams, collaborate as they jump onto the slippery slope of issues plaguing students labeled as needing "special education".

Breaking protocols of what might be considered politically correct, Carol and Belinda shed light on who these *Throw Away Kids* are and our obligation, as educators and parents, to turn the tide in their favor. *Throw Away Kids* are kids of every ethnicity and income range. They are the kids that need advocates to help them find their own voices and empower them as they move toward success.

Made in the USA
Columbia, SC
04 September 2020

18818523R00088